Discovering your Human Algorithm

How to Live with Meaning and Purpose

Zachary S. Brooks, PhD

Copyright

Discovering Your Human Algorithm

How to Live with Meaning and Purpose

By Zachary S. Brooks, PhD

ISBN: 9798645163136

Printed in the United States of America

Forewards

"Brilliant read! It would have been handy to use in my own degree module on coaching practices. I did a lot on bandura and coaching models. This would be useful for learning and progression practice, especially in sports such as taking steps 1 progression and purpose of a goal challenge to improve cement of life itself. Top work my friend!"

Stephen Jarvis
Winner of 22 medals (20) gold
5 world records at the World Transplant Games
Facebook: fb.com/stephen.jarvis.395

"Dr. Brooks strives for excellence in everything he does, which includes his "Dr. Z" Podcasts and his impressive professional endeavors. In Discovering Your Human Algorithm: How to Live with Meaning and Purpose you will learn not only how to live your life to the fullest, but also how to reach for your own personal human excellence."

Julia Seraphine
Entrepreneur and Social Media Expert
Facebook: fb.com/jewelz_stretermen
Instagram: instagram.com/sapphire._.eyes

"Dr. Brooks has achieved an unusually high degree of success in communicating well-researched and potentially complex concepts - in a conversational, enjoyable, inspirational and provocative manner. Wherever you are in your journey of self-discovery, understanding where passion is embraced, and success is achieved - you will find this book a worthy and valuable companion."

Mitch Pisik
Business Consultant and Executive Coach
Daily tweets on leadership:
Twitter@mitchpiski LinkedIn:
linkedin.com/in/mitchpisik

"Not everyone has their life figured out. We are continually searching to figure out what works best. In this book, you will find a road map based on an understanding of key values that contribute to our existential presence. This book breaks down the facets of life to a theorem that we can understand. If 1+1=2 and A+B=C, then the 6's As (Athletics, Adventure, Academics, Art, Advocacy, and The Human Algorithm) are logical parts to helping us create a "full" life. Through them, we can discover the essence of consciousness, humanness, and the notion of being that we are constantly seeking. This book, like Zach, is approachable. Zach inspires and motivates you to achieve your fullest potential."

Ms. Peta Leitermann-Long, MA, ABD
LinkedIn: linkedin.com/in/petalong
Twitter: @petalong

"I have known Zachary for many years, and it makes sense that he would be writing this book. Across the many roles he fulfills, Zach epitomizes living with meaning and purpose. Dr. Brooks has lived more lives than many of us ever will. The publication of his first book is a logical progression for him in this regard.

In my opinion as a clinical psychologist, Dr. Brooks is a human that has spent considerable time in self-reflection and personal growth which has cultivated a high level of contentment, achievement, social-connectedness, and personal meaning. "Discovering Your Human Algorithm" is an examination of the features--that every human possesses--that helped Dr. Brook's personal journey. If you interested in pursuing the 6A's, my impression is this book will be very helpful and interesting to you."

Ezra E Smith, PhD
Clinical Psychologist and Neuroscientist
ezra.e.smith at gmail.com

5

Preface

The birth of this book didn't happen overnight. It gestated for many years and finally took shape during my PhD studies with the help of a friend: Kate. I'd like to help others discover their own Human Algorithm through action. In particular, engaging in Athletics, Adventure, Academics, Art, and Advocacy in order to Discover Your Human Algorithm.

What this book is about?

The book is about discovering your best self and putting into action to improve life on earth for the 21st century.

Who are the target readers of this book?

The target readers are people who want to improve life on earth in the 21st century. Readers may be in self-discovery, creativity, and applied spirituality. The target readers age range is 20-70 who look forward to improving their inner and outer worlds.

Book Structure

After the introduction, there are six (6) chapters that help you Discover Your Human Algorithm. The chapters include Athletics, Adventure, Academics, Art, Advocacy, and The Human Algorithm. The final section includes some additional notes and links to exercises that you can follow to Discovering Your Human Algorithm and to live with meaning and purpose.

Acknowledgements

Reading acknowledgements has always been a curiosity of mine. Each document, book, or publication produces very nice words about very nice people. I always wondered about the connections between the acknowledger and acknowledgees.

How exactly was a father or mother inspirational? How exactly was the spouse supportive? How much of the work can be attributed to one's brilliance or stamina versus how much of the work can be attributable to those around the acknowledger?

The fact is that we inspire those around us daily and they inspire us. My speculations are wild. My acknowledgements are sincere.

I would like to acknowledge a few of the most important people in my life: my mother Nancy, my father Stephen, and my Beautiful Muse, Elena.

Dedication

I dedicate this book to wisdom. I dedicate this book to the use of wisdom to improve lives.

6A summary

1.   Athletics

To be human is to move.

2.   Adventure

To be human is to explore.

3.   Academics

To be human is to learn.

4.   Art

To be human is to create.

5.   Advocacy

To be human is to help others.

6.   The Human Algorithm

To be human is to improve the world.

Introduction

To be human is to begin.

When do you feel the most fulfilled? When do you feel a sweet equilibrium of your mind and spirit while doing an activity? Which moments do you look back on with the fondest sensations? Which moments do you look forward to the most?

Everyone has their own answers. I've asked myself these questions and for me I am the most fulfilled when I engage in one of the 6As of life – Athletics, Adventure, Academics, Art, Advocacy, and The Human Algorithm.

In the following pages, I'll share my definitions of each A but let's be clear.

Athletics is about movement, not being a professional athlete.

Adventure is about discovery and not necessarily extreme adventure.

Academics is about reflection and learning, not about getting a degree.

Art is about creation without a label.

Advocacy is about helping others without reward.

The Human Algorithm is about improving life processes on planet earth for the 21st century. It is the hardest to define but the most essential. It is a combination of the other A's, but it is wholly its own mist-like entity.

Discovering Your Human Algorithm captures the struggles and opportunities in our daily lives. As humans, we live one day to the next; analog. But our digital technologies give us the opportunity to create re-combinations of our lives daily. Technologies developed by our fellow humans present us with uncountable wonders but if we don't learn these wonders actively, then how can we live effectively?

Any wisdom in these pages is like finding a long-lost friend. Others have assessed the world and shared their wisdom before. I claim no special knowledge merely I seek to put an illuminating frame on human best practices in order to live life with meaning and purpose. The time to live with meaning and purpose is always now.

The first version of this book was called "The 6As: a practical philosophy for living life with meaning and purpose." The 6As are Athletics, Adventure, Academics, Art, Advocacy, and The Human Algorithm.

An Algorithm is defined as a process or set of rules to be followed in calculations or other problem-solving operations, especially by a computer. Algorithms have originally been created by humans to make computers better so why can't we use algorithms to live better? Discovering Your Human Algorithm should give you a process to follow to solve problems and discover yourself.

As you read, you will likely feel the influence of the "6As" throughout the book and I'm proud of that. However, the closer I arrived at publishing the book, I felt that the 6As didn't capture the essence of the book.

Essence is like a scent we take with us everywhere we go and to everyone we meet. Essence is like a scent we take away from everywhere we have been and from everyone we meet.

This essence, our 21st century Human Algorithm, will determine our individual and combined future. We are social animals. It is in our DNA to be social. Our approach to improving life on earth has to incorporate an individual and collective approach to solving problems and living life with meaning and purpose.

My qualifications

One of my early readers told me that he thought this book read more like an autobiography than a self-help book. I am working on a separate autobiography. Perhaps unconsciously the autobiography has cross fertilized Discovering Your Human Algorithm.

Another reader thought I should include more of my personal stories in the book. With my How to Algorithm podcast, I explore how people creatively craft lives on 21st earth. I will let you judge whether this book is too much or too little of an autobiography. Having undergone two kidney transplants has also give me some direct experience into life and the next. For me, the development of Discovering Your Human Algorithm derives from my life experiences, so I feel it is important to give some context.

Athletics. As a lifelong athlete, I played soccer in Europe as a teenager then soccer in college. I regularly compete in international triathlon competitions. Training and competing has given me numerous fundamental life lessons which is why I include it as a pillar of Discovering Your Human Algorithm.

Adventure. As a traveler, I have visited over 25 countries (a rookie by many standards) and learned four languages along the way. I have used anticipated regret to experience life and avoid regret. Every Adventure gives us an opportunity to experience something new but most importantly every Adventure leads to Discovering Your Human Algorithm.

Academics. As a learner, I earned a doctorate at the age when many people have had successful careers. I regularly learn new things such as writing a book because learning begets reflection, observation, and application. Everything we learn adds to our set of rules and just as importantly exceptions by which we can create our own optimized shortcuts (heuristics). Learning or Academics opens up you to Discovering Your Human Algorithm.

Art. As an artist, I've acted in Hollywood (for some Art and Hollywood together is an oxymoron) as a B-level actor (not good and not great), and I currently have numerous podcasts under the Dr. Z label. Creating something new awakens our spirit and gives us meaning and purpose. Whether your paint, dance, create YouTube

14

videos, crochet, or tend to a garden engaging in Art encourages Discovery Your Human Algorithm.

Advocacy. As an advocate, I have lobbied at the local, state, and federal levels on education and health care issues and I currently serve as a Trustee for the World Transplant Games Federation (wtgf.org). Helping others fundamentally underpins who we are. After all, we didn't birth ourselves. Our Mother, obviously, but also a team of people was there when you began. Helping others dignifies others and it dignifies our experiences and helps you Discover Your Human Algorithm.

The Human Algorithm. We can improve ourselves daily. In fact, we are required to do so. Our DNA discards that which does not serve us and our DNA preserves that which does serve us. The arrival of the Corona Virus Disease at the end of 2019, shortened to COVID-19, requires we adapt. The serum from survivors is being used to create new vaccines. Medical professionals and innovative biotech companies and organizations quickly respond by finding new ways to detect and treat those infected.

As a species, we have all the tools in place to treat COVID-19 but the question is whether we will be able to incorporate the new rules (social distancing, quarantines, online work, communication) into our Human Algorithm. The world flows with new technologies. Translational science turns laboratory discoveries into useable interventions. But these interventions can be slowed and disrupted by un-validated and mis-informed algorithms. We can program ourselves for the best. We can program ourselves for the worst. Let's choose the best for ourselves and others. Discovering Our Human Algorithm means smartly using technologies and adeptly interacting with them in the 21st century.

This book has been divided into six (6) chapters. Each chapter should be quickly readable during a morning, lunch, or evening break, or before bed. You can scroll through it while toggling on your phone or computer. Hopefully you can read it (or consume or ingest if you prefer) each part, consider it in the context

15

of your life, incorporate it, and move onto the next section. Or read it backwards. Always provide feedback through one of the many electronic means available such as DiscoveringYourHumanAlgorithm.com. Find the "How to Contact me" Section.

Learning

This book is dedicated to learning. As humans, we want to learn, and we want to learn how to learn better. From the moment a child falls after taking her/his first steps, then gets up, the child begins to learn. Of course, the learning predates this moment, but the effort of getting up after the fall is one of the first clear instances of learning.

When I finished my PhD and I was hooded1 in both the College of Science and the College of Humanities, I felt humbled by the honor. I felt humbled by the significance of carrying on the service and tradition of my academic forefathers (Dr. Linda Waugh, my academic mother who taught me about semiotics and language acquisition; Dr. Tom Bever, my academic father who taught me about psychology, language, and psycholinguistics; and someone you may have heard of before Dr. Noam Chomsky, my academic grandfather, who is known as a linguist, cognitive scientist, and political commentator).

When I finished my PhD, I felt very aware of the limits of my knowledge. It may sound strange that at the moment you receive a doctorate that you feel humbled by what you don't know but a wise man once said that "the only thing I know is that I don't know everything." It may sound very Tao in a twisted intuitive way, but the excitement of achieving the pinnacle of success at one of the leading universities in the world simply gave me a view of the next mountain, hidden by the clouds in the distance.

Learning is like that. It requires some amount of faith that when you apply yourself to the process somehow, someway you will find yourself speaking a new language, calculating a new formula, or building a home. It seems like magic, but is it?

1 The Hooding Ceremony is symbolic of passing the guard from one generation of doctors to the next generation of doctors. It's another way of saying "graduated" from the College of X. https://en.wikiversity.org/wiki/Hoodings

Why the 6As for Your Human Algorithm?

Since the foundation of Discovering Your Human Algorithm is grounded in learning, let's look at one clear visual model of learning. "U-Shaped Learning"1 explains in visual form how learning takes place. "U-shaped" learning refers to the letter "U." For the purposes of this conversation, let's give it three points. Point 1 is at the far-upper-left of the U. Point 2 is at lowest point of the U. Point 3 is at the far-upper-right part of the U (See image 1 below).

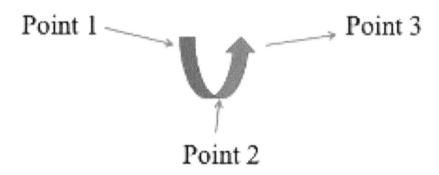

Image 1: Case (2005) Points on a U-Shaped curve.

Overall, learners exhibit strong learning before getting worse. It may be called beginner's luck. Starting at point 1, learners may feel an initial rush before descending to point 2 at the bottom of the

U. During the descent, effort may not feel as if it is leading to results. Learning feels cumbersome like putting on the wrong size of shoes. But when learners reach the bottom of the "U," their performance will gradually begin to improve (see graph 1 below). During the ascent, learners begin mastering the regularities and just as importantly the irregularities of the thing they are learning.

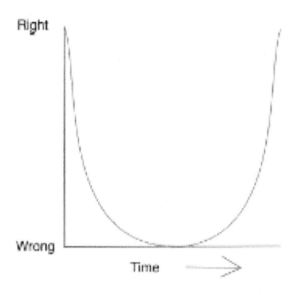

Graph 1: Case (2005) U-shaped learning curve that shows how learning gets worse before improving.

"U-shaped" learning is well demonstrated when someone learns a second language. For example, when people learn English as a second language, they learn various endings of verbs such as -ing, -ed, and -s. The -ing ending is used for progressive verb forms such as She is running, She is playing, and She is studying. The -ed ending is used for regular simple past verbs such as He worked, He studied, and He played. The -s ending is used for the third person in the simple tense such as She walks, She sings, and She smiles.

What do you think happens when people learning English come across these endings?2

At first, they learn the -ing ending and begin using it successfully (e.g. I am going, I am working, I am learning). They are at the top of the "U." Learning a new language at this phase can feel like the feel of riding a bicycle. You are free to explore a new space with a new tool.

What do you think happens when learners begin to acquire the -ed for the simple past?

Their accuracy of using -ing gets worse.

What happens when they begin to learn -s for simple present verbs?

Their accuracy of -ing gets even worse.

In fact, at this point learners have begun a nosedive as they are heading for the bottom of the "U." Nothing feels right. Every time they open their mouths, they feel like they are making a mistake and they may be right. They say things such as: I going, He talk, and They goed.3

So how do they get out of the bottom of the "U?" Here's a T.I.P.

Time. Intention. Persistence.

Over time learners gradually begin to notice the differences among -ing, -ed, and -s. It is at this point; learners begin their ascent up the "U" curve.4

With intention learners focus their attention on regularities and irregularities in the new language. For example, -ing follows words such as "am" "are" "is," "was," and "were."

Persistence allows the learner to continue on the tough days knowing that hard work pays off. Quitting isn't an option when learning.

The same "U-shaped learning" has been found with artistic skill, physical skill, and cognitive skill development.5 Learning to play an instrument, learning to lift weights, or learning new words follows the U-shaped trajectory.

Engaging in each of the A's – Athletics, Adventure, Academics, Art, and Advocacy – weekly or daily develops your Human Algorithm.

What about multiple "U's?"

Talking about learning one thing such as a new language is a useful approach to identify the steps of learning. However, learning is not a single process at a single moment in time. We learn multiple things at once. We can begin a semester by taking chemistry 101 (point 1) while simultaneously learning social media algorithms at a job we started before the semester began (point 2) and finishing a project we began a year ago (point 3). In this case, we have overlapping "U's" in which we are a beginner in one skill (fresh and excited), an intermediate learner (maximally frustrated) and a master (confidently applying a new skill to new situations). Traversing these many Us makes us surfers of life.

In fact, there are at least three types of learning.

1.   Learning

2.   Re-learning

3.   Unlearning

Learning means to acquire new knowledge or a skill. Re-learning means to learn again. Un-learning means to become aware of something you have learned, analyze it, and disassemble it.

Learning is both a process and a result. Learning may be difficult and pleasurable. Re-learning can be either laziness or mastery. Un-learning might be the most difficult because it requires awareness buried by our daily habits and hidden biases.

Of these, re-learning is the most frustrating process and the process that provides the most opportunities.

How often have you tried to teach yourself to learn a new programming language as a non-computer person? If you have tried and not succeed but then tried again you understand how frustrating re-learning can be. But re-learning is also an opportunity. How often do we have to remind ourselves that being polite in public is generally the best behavior to adopt or that honesty is the best policy is usually true in our relationships?

It is when we live our lives with multiple U's we live consciously with satisfaction because we need the pain of "failure" while descending one "U" in order to appreciate the ascent of another "U."

Discovering Our Human Algorithm allows us to be simultaneous experts and newbies which teaches us humility through dedication to process. The process imbued in each A are sufficiently challenging but not impossible. Simply engaging in the process as a learner focuses our time and attention in the moment.

Algorithms and Philosophies

An algorithm is defined as a process or set of rules to be followed to achieve a result. The word "algorithm" comes from a Persian mathematician named Muḥammad Khwarizmi. He lived primarily in Bagdad (present day Iraq) from 780-850. Muḥammad worked at the "House of Wisdom" (Dār al-Ḥikma). In the Latin alphabet, al-Khwarizimi became "algorithmi." Algorithms in computer programming and decision analysis provide its users a procedure to follow in order to solve problems.

Algorithms also help improve the procedures as the repeated use of them can show strengths and weaknesses in solution processes. These procedures can be modified by adding or subtracting variables. Algorithms make processes more efficient and consistent. Algorithms provide its users clear paths on how to improve.

So why can't we use algorithms to live better? Choosing the 6As as an Algorithm to follow can provide a path to living a life with meaning and purpose.

In a world of specialization, I have had a hard time specializing. There is such thing as a "generalist" and while its virtues are celebrated, a generalist is rarely paid. I love waking up at 5am to start training at 5:30am as much as any athlete enjoys waking up early to train. But I also love art which compels me to meet a different crowd late at night. I suspect many people have these overlapping interests.

I call Discovering Your Human Algorithm a practical philosophy. But is it a philosophy? Am I crazy to call an algorithm a philosophy?

After all, who cares about Kant while waking up to run?

What type of philosophy?

Philosophies can be broken down into five categories which include: Logic, Epistemology, Aesthetics, Ethics, and Metaphysics. Let's look at each. Logic is the study of good reasoning by examining the validity of arguments and documenting fallacies. It is likely this type of philosophy that pops into most people's minds. Epistemology is the study of the nature and scope of knowledge. It is also the type of philosophy you probably think about when you hear the word "philosophy." The next three categories may be a surprise. Aesthetics is the study of the nature of beauty, art, and taste, and the creation of personal kinds of truth. Ethics is the study of the right, the good, and the valuable. Finally, metaphysics is study of the state of being and the nature of reality.

Discovering Your Human Algorithm situates between aesthetics and ethics. The target audience for the book is focused on people who are creative and spiritual, but my goals are to be inclusive. Having been an outsider to countless groups and been the recipient of their exclusion, I offer suggestions, not prescriptions. I hope to include as many people as possible. Teammates know that everyone counts.

To count Discovering Your Human Algorithm as a philosophy, I use Scott H. Young's (Ultralearning, 2019) four criteria for life philosophies. The four criteria are: survival, happiness, meaning, and independence of circumstance.

Survival. Life philosophies require having sufficient basic needs such as food, shelter, and clothes. As more of these needs are met, our definition of "survival" can change, too. For example, having high-speed and consistent Wi-Fi is becoming a requisite for education and employment. As I write, the coronavirus is keeping much of the human population indoors yet social media is reflecting stories of humans exercising indoors, finding ways to create indoor adventures, learning online, creating humorous TikTok and YouTube videos, showing countless acts of altruism (thank you nurses, doctors, and medical care professionals), all the while learning how to improve life one moment at a time.

In this book, I intentionally use the words "fulfillment," "meaningful," "accomplishment," and "purpose." Just as success is a process more than a point, happiness is goal to strive towards especially during the depths of our suffering. This refrain comes from Victor Frankl's book, Man's Search for Meaning from 1984. People who are undergoing kidney dialysis treatment offer some of the best examples for the process of happiness while enduring daily suffering. Dallas, who had a kidney transplant, liked to compete in United States and World Transplant Games. But his kidneys failed again. Undeterred he kept riding his bike putting in over 3,000 miles of training one year. After he flipped over his handlebars during one ride, he thought he should go a little bit easier on the bike riding in case he got "the call" to receive a new kidney. He put his attention toward art and a year later he began exhibiting his works. While we can experience states of happiness, they are fleeting. But what remains consistent is the dedication to the process of happiness.

Happiness. Life philosophies should also provide happiness. It takes little more than a brisk walk to change one's mood. Planning your next vacation increases your immediate productivity. Learning something new will lead to a new mental journey. Coloring will take you away and fill you up with a sense of wonder. Reaching out to a friend will lift both of your spirits. Happiness can be fleeting because it can be detached from meaning. Meaning is the mental tick that gets you out of bed when you don't want to. It is the volunteer who receives nothing for her work except knowing that somehow and someway she may make her teammates feel better and help the "cause," "movement," or the "group" succeed.

Meaning. Life philosophies require that our daily activities connect to something greater. We need to be fulfilled and focusing on any of the As can lead to our desire and need to live meaningful lives. At the very least, the pursuit of mastery of any of the As gives us the chance to narrow our focus and to get feedback from that focus. With sustained efforts in -- Athletics, Adventure, Academics, Advocacy, Art, or The Human Algorithm -- we can create a sense of meaning and purpose for our lives. How often have you had a stressful day and at the end of decided to do something, sometimes anything, that made you happy? Suddenly, your frustrating day can be put into perspective. Practicing the 6As generates opportunities for meaning and purpose which are as important as food, water, and shelter.*

Belief in something greater and belief in contribution is a central tenant to meaning. John awakes early to volunteer on behalf of a medical cause. He works day and night because he believes in advancing the cause. Attention seekers often burn out because their effort was derived from attention for short-term benefit rather than for long-term meaning. People who believe in a cause generate unlimited energy for themselves and others because they have found meaning in the effort.

Independence of Circumstance. Life philosophies need to function in all circumstances. The 6As require movement, discovery, learning, creativity, and assistance of any type. That means that the standard is simply action, any action, toward a life with meaning and purpose daily. At 17, Karen sat in a wheelchair as she went to her prom. Her survival, happiness, and meaning were central to her life even if her pursuit of these activities had to be modified.

A Human Algorithm example

Angel is a doctoral student in public health. She reads, writes, analyzes documents, and checks about 100 emails daily. For many people, this would take up all their time, but not for Angel. She starts her day by running and often takes pictures of the sunrise as it peaks over the mountain. At night, she plays guitar, plans trips around the world, works on a book all the while planning for her next marathon. Her average speed per mile is 7:15 which means it takes her about 3 hours and 10 minutes to finish a marathon. 7:15 is 3 minutes faster than other women in age group (25-29). By itself, it is impressive, but Angel's impressiveness doesn't end there. She always has had a sense of fairness so recently when she was sexually assaulted, she fiercely advocated for herself in a system stacked against her. She began calling attorneys nationwide. She is constantly busy7 and she is constantly improving her ability to read people and situations, and she is practicing her Human Algorithm in multiple languages.

Discovering Your Human Algorithm and practicing the 6As requires conscious living. It requires a dedication to curiosity. In the book Flow: The Psychology of Optimal Experience, Mihaly Csikszentmihalyi (Me-hal-ee Chik-sent-Mihal-yi) shares that people are happier when they are engaged in activities that combine challenge and skill in an optimal balancing act. Each of the 6As offers people to engage with their level of curiosity and skill to challenge themselves.

Is it more satisfying to complete in Kona's Ironman Triathlon or to walk once around the track after receiving a heart transplant? The answer is likely that they are equally satisfying athletic experiences because each person followed their curiosity, created a personal challenge, then achieved their goal. To move is to be. To move is the predecessor to all As.

It is not that Angel's life is without challenges, but it is through dedicated curiosity that Angel finds fulfillment and happiness.

How to Live with Meaning and Purpose

How questions impart power. How do you discover your meaning and purpose? Action.

Everyone likes to binge watch their favorite shows and everyone has the choice to find meaning and purpose now! Engaging in the 6As can help you with your survival, happiness, and meaning because no matter your circumstances you have it within your power to practice. It is important to set goals, work to achieve them, be humble about your accomplishments, and then when you feel down, reset your goals so that they are optimally* difficult. Athletics, Adventure, Academics, Art, Advocacy, and The Human Algorithm take just a few minutes daily.

Let's get started.

----

1 "U-shaped learning" also called "U-shaped development" has been used in … and applied linguistics.

2 Kwon (2005), Brown (1973), Dulay & Burt (1973), Lightbown (1974).

3 If the mistakes sound similar to mistakes child make when they are learning English, you're correct. Children often overuse -ed (goed, knowed, gived) while they are learning the correct irregular forms (went, knew, gave).

4 Murakami & Alexopoulou (2016) have found that there is variation in learning based on someone's first language.

5 Davis, Jessica (1997)

6 Bennett, Milton J. "Intercultural communication: A current perspective." Basic concepts of intercultural communication: Selected readings (1998): 1-34.

7 Angel doesn't consider any of her 6A activities "work."

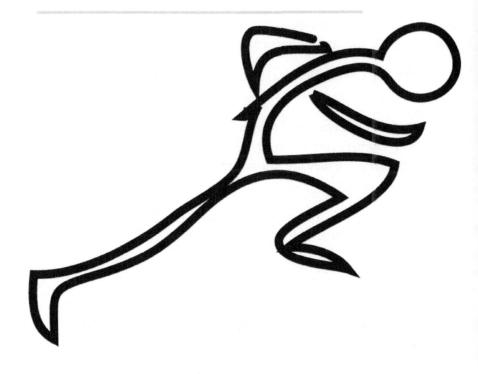

Athletics

To be human is to move.

As humans, we are born to move.

With movement comes possibilities.

Athletics is the key to all other As. We cannot discover, learn, create, help others, or improve if we don't move. Athletics is not about being an athlete. Athletics means we use the most human tool we have: our bodies. When we are moving, we are fully exploring ourselves as humans.

Athletics for everyone

.One foot in front of the other. That's all he had to do. That's all that anyone else has to do. He had already finished 50 meters. Just 50 meters to go. The crowd grew louder. Johnny allowed himself to look up for a split second to see people standing and cheering. He couldn't help himself. He hadn't heard this many people cheer since he left the hospital a year ago. While Johnny enjoyed the cheers, at the same time, his father, Stan, had a terrifying realization. It had been a mistake to allow Johnny to look up. He pulled a little tighter on Johnny's back brace to find the right height. Johnny squeezed more concentration into every step of his specially-fitted walker adored with his team colors. Just two more minutes his father thought. Just two more minutes to walk 50 meters.

Most people can walk 100 meters in a minute or less. But for Johnny running like this took a massive effort, not to mention the help of his father. When he was two, he received an emergency heart transplant and now five years later, he had just now begun to walk. The Transplant Games motivated him to move, to compete, and to celebrate his existence.

The first of the 6As is Athletics. We wouldn't be alive but for movement of sperm and egg. Our cells and our entire body are constantly in movement. From our first steps, we move. The goal of our movement is not always important. The act itself is always important. After surgery, doctors, nurses, and others implore us to "move!" "Ambulatory," is the word. Whether you walk 10 steps or more, doctors know that movement helps recovery and stave off other illness.

Movement is fundamental to your social life as well. The first time you walked to school with a friend, you noticed how you synchronize your steps. Movement leads to cooperation but at some point, your friend seems to be walking a little bit faster. You quicken your pace to keep up, but then you notice that you pass your friend. Movement leads to competition. Movement among humans is dynamic.

If you have ever walked on a crowded street, you know how dynamic all of us have to be to avoid bumping into each other and to reach our destinations. When we think of Athletics most of us imagine a professional basketball a football player, an Olympic swimmer, a gymnast, or an ice skater. Or maybe we imagine the United States women's soccer team, the Russian national hockey team, or the All Blacks Rugby team from New Zealand. In this book I take a more general view of Athletics. To be human is to move.

First Olympics

As a baker, Koroibos1 must have had a rush of thoughts before the start of the race. Maybe he wondered if the person who was looking after his kitchen was using just the right mix of flour, water, salt, and yeast. Were they accurate in their measurements or were they, as was their habit, just tossing in ingredients haphazardly? Were they taking the time to knead the bread in order to release the gas holes that formed during the rising process? Were they taking the bread out of the oven at the correct time or were they letting it burn because they were distracted playing "knucklebones"2. Were they letting it cool long enough or were they shoving their hands inside the warm bread?

None of that mattered now as he stepped up to the starting line. He focused on keeping his breath calm which was hard because one of the other competitors like to take deep breaths and blow out loudly when he came to the starting line. All that mattered now was ....

.... running ... faster and faster. His life was transformed in 100 milliseconds. He ran in an out-of-body state. To prove that the people from Elis, Greece were special, he ran. He ran to honor Zeus.

One step after another and he could feel himself slowly surely gain distance on his rivals. In just a few seconds, he might ...

... win ...

... as he crossed the line, he become temporarily blind. In his absolute focus on the finish line, all Koroibos could hear was the pounding steps of his competitors that he mistook for wild horses ...

... as his heart rate began to drop, he looked up at the blue sky and saw a lonely cloud looking for a friend but the friend he saw was a stranger approaching holding out his hand.

... Koroibos won. His mind went blank. The trill of winning took over which he couldn't comprehend. The same person who shook his hand then offered him an olive wreath as his prize.

When Koroibos finally had a conscious moment, he looked around for his fellow competitors, the people who understood this moment better than anyone. Most had begun to saunter away from the pitch. He touched the backs of a couple of them to extend the moment and to connect with others. Still, by winning Koroibos stood alone as the first Olympic Champion in 776 B.C. or nearly 2,800 years ago.

Between performance and injury

To prepare for a competition, amateurs and professionals alike push their bodies to their limits. The margin of error is very small because when you push too much you can get injured but if you don't push yourself enough you can't achieve the physical and mental strength in order to win.

For modern Olympic, professional, and high-end amateur athletes, there is a fine line between preparing to give a top-level performance and having a career-threatening injury. Knowing this reality is like knowing there is a ticking time bomb inside of you. Ignore. You have to push through.

How often in life have you been overwhelmed? Maybe you have two kids in the backseat, one is crying and sick, the other seems fine but she's been quieter than usual. Meanwhile, you teach class in 30 minutes and you're supposed to drop off the kids and you are praying the babysitter isn't late today because you have to pick up the recital dress at the dry cleaner's that was ruined when your child threw up because of eating too much candy. When will you have time to prepare for the class you're supposed to teach today?

Anything can go wrong. Yet you continue.

The first A of Athletics teaches us to continue despite our frustrations. You may have crashed during the bike race and despite the setback you get back up to finish the race. Despite the setbacks, you finish the chores, the things you set out to do.

Athletics can teach us the two secrets of success for life and it is the cornerstone to Developing Your Human Algorithm.

1.   Take the first step,
2.   Keep walking.

What if something does go wrong? How to comeback from an injury

When you get injured or when you have to take time off after an illness, you have to strategize your comeback. You have to find out how to get back to the same fitness level without rushing. One method that works is working out by yourself. A cyclist can sign up for a time trial event. A runner can sign up for a 5k and run a slower place. A karateka (a person who practices karate) can run through the entire routine, perhaps a little slower, and perhaps can avoid any contact drills (there are often zero contact drills during a karate session).

A large portion of the population will be coming back from social isolation due to the coronavirus in 2020 or possibly 2021. If you fall into this category, try to take a little more time to ramp up your workouts. As my friend says, it's just a minor setback before a major comeback.

In my own life, I have had to start again after two major surgeries and multiple hospitalizations. I always get frustrated and a bit angry, but some way I "step through" the anger. That's what I call it, stepping through. What I mean is that my anger has a life of its own. It's going to last for a set period of time. I don't always know how long but I know I can't wait for my anger to dissipate to accomplish my daily goals. Anger, for me, feels like a mist, I step through it taking some of the anger with me but the farther I go the less I feel it and the more I can shake it off.

Athletics extends and improves life

By now you know, exercise extends and improves life. But engaging in exercise requires consistency. You can't take too many days off and you can't over train. In other words, choosing Athletics as a part of your lifestyle requires an "optimum range" of activity. After all there are also five other As to consider.

How do you know what is optimal? Optimal is defined as the "best" or "most favorable" point, degree, or amount. This is obviously open to interpretation without some guidelines, but it is the amount of effort you exert that gives you the most benefit without deleting from that benefit. In biology, "range of tolerance" refers to the range of environmental conditions that are tolerable for survival in a species. In sociology, the range of tolerance is the scope of behaviors considered acceptable by society.

In both biology and sociology, we can push the boundaries, but we may push those boundaries with a cost. Dr. Nieman codified the idea of overtraining into the "J-curve" to describe the relationship between exercise intensity and the risk of acquiring upper respiratory tract infections (URTI). What is your optimal level of daily exercise?

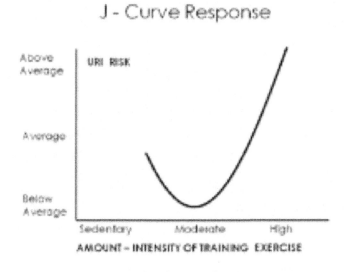

Graph 1: J-Curve of exercise, exercise intensity, and risk (Nieman, 1990)

Mirror Neurons

In every culture, there are prescribed movements passed down from one generation to the next. Think about the men's or women's World Cup. Teams approach the same game with 1 ball, 2 goals, and 22 players from varying perspectives. Cultures offer various views of what's possible in dance. This is similar to people passing down grammar from one generation to the next. Kids learn words and when they begin school, they start to learn formally prescriptive grammar. The same thing goes with movements. We pass along our movements through demonstration, observation, practice, and feedback. The neural mechanisms that support the learning of movement are called "mirror neurons."

A mirror neuron is a neuron that fires both when an animal acts and when the animal observes. When we observe actions of others, our mirror neurons perform the same action, at least cognitively, by "mirroring" the behavior of the people we observe. Think about watching your favorite sporting event. At the end of a long competition, do you ever feel exhausted as a fan? Maybe it is because you were participating in the competition with your mirror neurons. For Athletics, you can motivate and inspire others to their best when you do your best because of mirror neurons.

Athletics in your daily life

How do you include movement in your daily life? How about including 21 minutes and 43 seconds of movement daily? The American Heart Association recommends getting 150 minutes per week of moderate-intensity aerobic activity. 21 minutes and 43 seconds is nearly exactly the same amount of time as the average sitcom on television, Netflix, Hulu, Amazon Prime, or other online platforms. You could combine watching your favorite sitcom with exercise.

To be human is to move.

To move is the first step to Discovering Your Human Algorithm.

----

1 Koroibos was a Greek baker and athlete who won the first recorded Ancient Olympic Games race in 776 BC.

2 This was a game that used ankle-bones of goats or sheep which was similar to jacks or five stones. Jacks or five stones is played when a player throws five stones into the air with one hand and tries to catch as many as possible on the back of the same hand.

Adventure

To be human is to explore.

As humans, we are born to explore

With movement comes risk. With movement comes reward.

About 100,000 years ago homo sapiens from modern-day Ethiopia began to wonder: What if there are more resources over there? By over there, the hunter-gatherer tribes still meant to stay nearby. On average, this group of homo sapiens traversed about 54 steps per day, or about two or three houses away from yours. It's your neighbor's neighbor. After a week, the same people might have traveled 300 meters which is three-fourths the length of a track, or about 2-3 blocks of an American city. Just by venturing to your neighbor's house, in the course of 1,000 years you and your great-grand parents (30 generations) walked about 8,700 miles. That is like going from Los Angeles to New York, then New York to Seattle, then Seattle to Atlanta.

Slowly but predictably wondering becomes wandering.

Whether Adventure started out of a sense of desperation or innovation, humans have moved. Each new block, city, and region offers a new challenge and it begins with what if?

It is through taking action with some unknown results that gives us the chance to learn about ourselves and others. Extending ourselves one standard deviation1 away from the norm is an Adventure that is more likely to transform our perspective leading to living life with meaning and purpose.

Adventure Formula

Let's put adventure into a formula.

Action

Time

Our wondering and wandering ancestors simply input action into time. In our individual lifetimes, it is the action put into time that creates Adventure. If you drive the same route to work every day over time you will experience a lower sense of Adventure as the details of the route fade into routine. If you vary your transportation modalities and walk, ride your bike, take ride shares, or use public transportation, then you will experience a higher sense of Adventure because your action over time will differ.

Your choice of action (call it "x") over the same time (call it "y") helps determine your Adventure.

In the dictionary, Adventure is defined as an unusual and exciting, typically hazardous, experience or activity." As a verb, Adventure is defined as engaging in a hazardous and exciting activity, especially the exploration of unknown territory.

And that's what makes the second "A" so amazing. Adventure can be created by anyone at any time with a simple change of outlook. For any Adventurer, often the most difficult moment of day is getting out of bed. What is so powerful about the second "A" is that embedded in each Adventure is a problem waiting to be explored and solved. The formula works similar to the first.

Action

Problem

If action is applied to a problem, then solving the problem becomes more likely. But what also becomes more likely is stumbling across a new discovery! The decision to act toward a goal creates Adventures of our choosing. The rewards for the majority of our Adventures is a greater sense of satisfaction. Adventure compresses time. At least, experiencing Adventure creates the impression of more time because more of your brain has to engage with the new experience compared to engaging in a similar experience every day. Travel is usually what people associate with Adventure and often people return from travel refreshed because not only have they applied action to time, but they have also applied action to solving problems both of which can be frustrating experiences during the moment, but add so much to our lives after the moment. After travel, we can return to our routine with a new perspective which itself is another form of Adventure. This leads to a new formula.

New perspective

Time

When we apply new perspectives to time, we can see the world differently. With both the action/time and action/problem formulas, one key element is adaptation. It is the hidden ingredient in both formulas because it comes very naturally when we give ourselves to Adventure. Our bodies and brains adjust and modify to make the processes suitable for us. The threshold for "suitable" can differ for everyone but simply by taking the first step we increase our sense of Adventure and sense of purpose.

Applying action to time quickly helps you *Discover Your Human Algorithm.*

Adventure, Adaptation, and Staying Ahead of the curve

In the book Adaptive Leadership, authors Alexander Grashow and Ronald Heifetz (2009) borrow from evolutionary biology which has three parts: preserve, discard, and create.

Successful adaption requires that we preserve DNA essential for our survival. At a behavioral level, when we enter into a new Adventure, we preserve virtually everything that makes us unique. This is critical for survival. When we go to a job interview, we endeavor to show our best selves, but fundamentally we have to be ourselves, otherwise the interviewers will notice a lack of authenticity. It is crucial that we recognize and preserve ourselves for whatever the Adventure.

Successful adaptation also requires discarding DNA that no longer serves the species' needs. Similarly, during Adventures we have to discard our behaviors that don't help us in our Adventures. Watch any reality television show such as Survivor and you can see for yourself when someone's stubbornness, when unconquered, can lead to a quick dismissal from the island. Think about a time you found yourself in a new place. Sometimes the routine developed in your daily behavior is counterproductive. You may have to temporarily discard a habit in order to achieve a certain goal.

Successful adaptation also means that we create new DNA arrangements in order to flourish. When we preserve and discard, we are ready for the next challenge because we have created a new way to view things. Think of a rookie quarterback who comes into the National Football League cocky and ready to conquer. Only when he has preserved his belief in himself, discarded behaviors that don't help him or the team succeed, will he be ready to succeed having created a new arrangement of self.

If you want to take only three things away from this book, learn the principles of preserve, discard, and create to Discover Your Human Algorithm.

Adventure and Regret

One line of decision-making research is the study of regret. Regret is an emotion. But regret differs from other emotions such as anger, happiness, jealousy, and sadness because it is primarily a cognitive-based emotion. Regret often means that the simple thought of an event can trigger an emotion. Regret also differs in another key aspect. It can be applied before or after an event. Though regret is usually seen as an emotion that looks backwards it can also be used to look forward. In other words, we can use regret to assist us with possible decisions and outcomes. This is called anticipated regret. This form of regret can help us avoid bad decisions and/or make decisions that reward us.

For example, if a man had too much drink one night and then felt bad the next day, he may eventually use anticipated regret to drink less or not drink at all. If a woman decided not to apply for a position, then felt bad about not applying, the next time she may use anticipated regret to apply for the job. In both cases, the decision makers are trying to avoid a negative emotion in the future.

The same thinking can be used in Adventures. Michael and William both worked in a Silicon Valley startup where the expected work hours were at least 11 hours daily. It was also expected that employees work on Saturdays. Both Michael and William also loved to play golf. They constantly looked for the best deals on the best courses. Courses typically offered the best tee times and rates during slower days, like Mondays.

One Sunday night William called Michael with a proposal. If we skip tomorrow, we can play Poppy Ridge Golf Course for half price. Michael responded that if they missed work then everyone would wonder where they were, and it would be hard to earn back the social capital in offices where every extra minute of work count.

In other words, Michael was using an anticipated regret argument of not going to work. William countered by saying, "in ten years do you think we will remember an extra day of work or do you think I'll remember how well you hit a 5 iron on the 12th hole?" William was also using an anticipated regret argument of not going golfing. Both used an anticipated regret argument. Michael wanted minimize problems at work. William wanted to maximize pleasure.

At the end, they decided to go because they had never taken a day off and they both realized that in the long term, they would regret missing a day at work less than missing a day on a premium golf course at half price.

Most people engage in cost-benefit analyses such as these in which they weigh the strengths and weaknesses of alternative choices. Adventure seekers use the cost-benefit analysis of anticipated regret which follows the same pattern as William and Michael's conversation.

If I do X, I will feel Y and if I don't do X, I will feel Z.

Researchers at Tilburg University and Utrecht University in The Netherlands found people regret things they didn't attempt more than the things they attempted (Zeelenberg, van den Bos, van Dijk, 2002). In other words, it is generally better to try and fail than to not try at all. This pattern of regret was found to be stronger after previous inaction that led to negative outcomes. If sitting on the couch doesn't produce the outcome you want, doesn't trying the alternative make sense?

Given this data on trying and regretting less, one approach may be to make decisions so that you won't regret later even when unsure about the outcome. How often do students choose one major then change it? Answer: often. During the first couple of years of college, students often change their minds about their studies. While time and money are factors in students' decisions during college for economic reasons, the students are using anticipated regret to avoid regretting something larger later.

Anticipated regret also has health benefits. Researchers at the University of North Carolina and at Harvard University found that anticipated regret has a positive association with future healthy behaviors (Brewer, DeFrank, Gilkey, 2016). That is, thinking about a future feeling of exercising, or not, can affect today's decision to exercise. In other words, when you're unsure if you want to exercise, think about how you will feel later, then make your decision.

The next time you consider undertaking an Adventure be it large or small consider using anticipated regret. Your future self will thank you.

Adventure: be an optimal hero

Beyond avoiding regret, deciding to embark on an Adventure brings visceral, heart-pounding, and life-changing rewards, risks, and possible injury. But most people no matter how they define Adventure aim for an optimal Adventure experience.

In 1986, Martin and Priest developed the Adventure Experience Paradigm (see diagram below) to capture "peak adventure" and adventures that vary from the optimal experience. "Peak adventure" is achieved at "the point at which personal competence matches and balances with situational risk." This is important for 6A people because your personal competence may be higher or lower so concentrating on matching your desires, skills, and experience for Adventure should guide you. If you want to do a bike race, it's probably a good idea to ride your bike around your neighborhood and do some group rides first.

Graph 1: The Adventure Experience Paradigm (Martin & Priest, 1986), a model of the adventure experience.

44

The Adventure Experience Paradigm has five (5) phases. In phase one, Exploration and Experimentation, the task is easy which is a good time to try new things. Your skill level is high for the low-risk challenge. This is fun phase for most people, and it should be an important touchstone phase for anyone who wants to pursue Adventure because there are few things as sweet as learning without repercussions.

In phase two, Adventure, the task provides people an experience with some risk and an uncertain outcome. It is as this point that the difficulty of the task and one's individual competence are nearly aligned. One's skill may be slightly greater than the difficulty of the task or the difficulty may be slightly more than one's skill, but it is the fine-line balance that creates enough friction for excitement.

In phase three, Peak Adventure, the difficulty of the task is equal to the skill of the individual. Looking for this equilibrium and then experiencing it is one of the greatest motivators for Adventures. At this point, people often find themselves hooked on Adventure because the thrill from this experience spills over to the rest of their life. The fleeting moment that defines the Adventure is sought out again and again.

In phase four, Misadventure, the difficulty of the task is either greater than the skill of the individual or it is perceived as such. Sometimes misadventure takes place because of the immediate negative reactions. The challenges in Misadventure may be also outside of one's control (social, emotional, physical, or financial). For example, if someone normally skis on a moderately difficult mountain at an inexpensive ski resort, but then is invited to ski on extremely difficult mountain at an expensive ski resort, the increase in difficulty may be too large. Even if the person has the skills for the challenge, the expense of the trip may turn an Adventure into a Misadventure. Even if the person can afford the challenge, the difficulties on the new slope may create a Misadventure. We often slip into Misadventure unaware. Recognizing the mis-match and adapting quickly become valuable skills.

In phase five, Devastation and Disaster, the difficulty is far greater than one's skill to the point where someone can experience major injury or death. It is not a situation that people want to encounter. What is strange about phase five, however, is that while it is the least frequent of all Adventures, it is often the Adventure people imagine in order to avoid undertaking an action.

The explanation comes from the availability bias. What's that? Let's ask and answer some questions first.

Cars or planes?

Roofers or Border Patrol agents?

Cows or Sharks?

Of these pairs which one is more deadly? Don't look up the answers. Just say your first instinct answer out loud.

Cars or planes?

Roofers or Border Patrol agents?

Cows or Sharks?

Most people would say flying is more dangerous than driving, being a Border Patrol agent is more dangerous than being a roofer, and sharks are more deadly than cows. In each case, those answers are incorrect. Why? Because of the Availability Bias which is the tendency to overestimate the likelihood of events with greater "availability" in memory. If a memory is recent, unusual, or emotional, it is likely to be more available and more usable to make decisions.

Available doesn't always mean accurate, however. The next time you hear of a major event on the news, pause to avoid falling into the trap of what is easily available. Take a second to think about the risk of your possible new Adventure. Is your new Adventure truly risky or is it worth trying a new activity?

Adventure in your daily life

How do you include explorations in your daily life? If you're stuck at home to help flatten the curve of coronavirus infections, you can visit online museums, plan your next vacation, or join a bicycle ride on Swift. Whatever you do, you can choose to see life as an Adventure. The 6As are designed to give your clear ideas and actions to live with meaning and purpose. Apply action to time to create your own new Adventure daily.

To be human is to explore.

To explore is the second step to Develop Your Human Algorithm.

----

1 In statistics, the standard deviation is a measure that is used to quantify the amount of variation of a set of data values. A low standard deviation indicates that the data points tend to be close to the, while a high standard deviation indicates that the data points are spread out over a wider range of values. https://en.wikipedia.org/wiki/Standard_deviation

Academics

To be human is to learn.

As humans, we are born to learn.

With adventure comes observation and study.

For this book, Academics is defined as learning in all of its forms. The order of Academics after Athletics (movement) and Adventure (discovery) deserves an explanation.

Many of our body's movements are involuntary governed by our Automatic Nervous System (ANS). These movements regulate our heart rate, digestion, respiratory rate, urination, and sexual arousal. Whether we a newly born or nearly dead, the ANS ensures movement which is why Athletics for the 6A philosophy must come first.

Next is Adventure, motivated movement. According to Eric A. Walle (2016), a developmental psychologist at the University of California Merced, the beginning of walking is a developmental phase that "sets in motion a cascade of change across a range of domains, including social interactions and language learning."[1] Infants begin crawling between the ages of 6 and 10 months about the same time that infants begin developing consciousness (Kouider et al., 2013).[2] It is through movement that a child begins to interact with the world and develop its personality. During this phase, babies begin to learn basic sounds, discriminating one language from another.

Given the natural order of learning to crawl while learning language, it is seems natural that the order should follow the human experience. Repeating this pattern is one of the secrets to Discovering Your Human Algorithm.

Academics refers to reflecting on Adventures, learning, and applying learning to new situations.

Like Athletics, a person does not have to be a formal academic. Rather, Academics refers to reflecting on an action, a mental activity, or an emotion and trying to learn from that experience and apply it to a new situation.

Language Equals Human

Since learning is a central tenet to this book, then language is central to what makes us human. Language is the most dominating of all modalities. When we talk about learning, attention, memory, reasoning, and decision making it is usually assumed we are talking about the use of language to make these mental operations possible. The use of language is so intertwined with our brains that it is hard to imagine the non-use of language.

Think about it. Even when you are engaged in a non-verbal task you probably engage in an internal dialogue to assist you. For example, when you navigate a new park, you don't necessarily need to use language to orient yourself with directions or landmarks. But the next time you go to a park try not to use language to assist your navigation.

The ability to recognize faces is also a non-verbal task. We don't need to know language to recognize faces but try to not use language to help you remember someone's face. Invariably the person's name will be at the tip-of-your tongue. Recognizing a song by its first few bars or measures doesn't require language but try not to recognize the song without naming it.

Finally, think about the role that language plays in solving math problems. In a study of deaf Nicaraguan children who had taught themselves sign language Spaepen (2011) found something fascinating between children who had learned at home versus children who had learned at school. The children who learned at home had a hard time understanding numbers larger than three because they didn't have the language to develop or grasp numbers. The students at school had been taught numbers and the language used for numbers.

Noam Chomsky calls the study of human language the "human essence." It is homo sapiens whose vocal tract anatomy permit the production of sounds that can be coded as speech.

It is the development of this skill that set us on our path 50,000 years ago. The ability to produce physical signals, collect them, organize them, and share them with one another to create concrete and abstract realities underpins our lives.

But what is Academics?

The definition found in dictionary.com for Academics relates to study that is theoretical but not necessarily practical. With this in mind, let's look at two types of research: 1. Basic Research and 2. Applied Research.

Basic Research is often thought of as theoretical and universal that adds to human knowledge. While basic research adds to human knowledge it often does not have an immediate practical application. This leads to criticisms about funding academia and research. After all, why fund, things that offer no immediate value?

In 1960, Professor Dan Kleppner's goal was not to invent a useful technology. In fact, his goal had no immediate practical value. Instead his goal was to study General Relativity which is the geometric theory of gravitation published by Albert Einstein in 1915. In essence, 50 years after one of Einstein's discoveries Kleppner and his colleagues wanted to understand General Relativity through the invention of an atomic clock. Why? Just because.

Just because is often the answer to the question "why study that?"

It turns out the atomic clock, however, was fundamental to the creation of global positioning system (GPS) technology. Can you imagine your life without a GPS? It is used in aviation, farming, marine sciences, surveying, the military, financial services, telecommunications, heavy vehicle guidance, road transportation, and of course your phone.

Another way to think about basic research is to think about your own life and how you click through various Wikipedia pages. The only driving force behind your clicks is simple curiosity. What new ideas do you have while clicking aimlessly about various topics that stoke your curiosity? Discovering Your Human Algorithm requires your curiosity and curiosity is the precursor to inventive thought.

Dr. Smoot (2006) says, "People cannot foresee the future well enough to predict what's going to develop from basic research. If we only did applied research, we would still be making better spears." The takeaway from basic research is that it always has value even if not immediate.

Applied Research is often thought of as practical. It adds to an existing human technology or technique. After all, we have to solve problems. For example, numerous advances in the 20th century were developed because of the improvement of sanitation systems around the world. From the Greeks to the Egyptians to the Chinese and Americans, sanitation systems solved a real and immediate problem that allowed people to live better and longer.

The world of clinical psychology is full of applied research. Antidepressants were initially created to treat allergies. Over time, doctors found incidentally that people with symptoms of depression also improved. Doctors began to use medications to treat allergies to treat depression. Even though the doctors were using applied research to solve one problem, they discovered that the medications had the potential of solving an additional problem. Through this iterative3 process applied research can bear on basic research.

At this point, you may have noted that distinctions between basic research and applied research may seem odd. We can analyze basic and applied research as if they are part of a sequence. But perhaps applied and basic research simply represent two parts on a continuum.

If we operationalize that basic research comes before applied research or that applied research comes before basic research, then we can develop a mental model that may prevent us from seeing the connections. In decision making, the most fundamental bias is called the "confirmation bias." In this bias, we interpret new information in order to confirm our existing bias.

To be learners, we have to want to learn but also, we need to be aware of how our current thinking may limit our ability to see new ways of thought.

That is one day proceeds another. But our connections are like double-sided Legos that can fit together in various directions. Seeing the multidirectional fit of our multisided lives is one of the fundamental benefits of the digital world. Digital is not only a technology of 1's and 0's it is a metaphor through which we create new metonymies4 and meanings.

Part of academic thinking is holding multiple thoughts together simultaneously. For me, the magic word is "AND." Reflect on your own life AND the relationships within it. You love your partner AND your partner annoys you. Your job brings you joy AND it takes all of your time. Spending money allows you to have a product or experience AND it means you have to give up on another product or experience.

How to learn?

As I have shared before there are three types of learning – learning, re-learning, and un-learning – but still the question remains: what does it mean to learn something?

From dictionary.com, learning is defined as "the process of acquiring new, or modifying existing, knowledge, behaviors, skills, values, or preferences." In other words, learning requires a change from A to B which requires movement (Athletics) and trying things differently (Adventure).

So how to learn?

According to Professor Kate Sweeny in 2018, the answer lies in playing more video games. In other words, engaging in activities that allow you to pass time more quickly and pleasantly conduces learning. When engaged, we achieve a 'flow state.' Being engaged in a process, such as a video game, reduces people's stress and increases more positive emotions. Still, the participants couldn't just play any video game. The video games used in the experiment had to be optimally difficult for the participants. The game had to be just hard enough to keep participants' attention, to improve their skills (x+1), and it had to be intrinsically motivating.

In other words, just like Adventure your skills and the challenge have to optimally aligned in order to create an enjoyable learning experience.

How to learn quicker?

Given that most of us feel obliged to do more things, i.e. multitask, is there a way to learn quicker? If we could learn quicker, perhaps we could improve the quantity of our learning and the quality of our lives.

Researchers Wymbs, Bastian, and Celnik (2016) found that "if you practice a slightly modified version of a task you want to master, you actually learn more and faster than if you just keep practicing the exact same thing multiple times in a row." For example, if you learn to play an instrument and you alter your practice sessions between playing the instrument slightly louder/softer or faster/slower you will learn quicker. When doing Athletic training, those who make slight variations to their workouts in terms equipment, duration, or intensity learn quicker than those who continue with the same routines. In other words, learning is amplified when forced to adapt.

Academics in the age of distractions

As you are reading this book or listening to me narrate this book, you are likely distracting yourself. You may have read that people are not good at multitasking. Still, you work to disprove that science daily. If you are like me, you have two browsers open with at least 20 tabs. While you are reading, you may be toggling between apps on your phone, texting, and double-tapping an Instagram post.

Does this mean that the process of learning differs from previous generations? Yes and No.

Yes. Blasiman, Larabee, and Fabry (2018) studied the effect of six distractions on learning (folding laundry, playing a computer video game, texting on a cell phone, engaging in a conversation, watching a low-arousal video, and watching a high-arousal video). Students were asked to learn a task while distracted. Then they were tested on what they learned. How do you think they performed compared to when they were not-distracted?

They scored as low as 62% and as high as 87% on tests. Think about it. A brilliant learner demonstrates only 62% of his or her ability when distracted.

Does this mean that the process of learning differs from previous generations?

No. There have always been distractions to learning. The tonic for distractions has always been concentration on one task. When it comes to learning in the age of distractions, the formula is simple. Reduce distractions and increase concentration.

Academics in your daily life

How do you include learning in your daily life? One way is simple. Ask yourself every morning, "what will I learn today?" Your brain will spend the day answering that question and giving you results. Academics like the other As shouldn't been seen as a pastime reserved for the few. Just as amateur athletes don't stop exercising simply because they are not professional athletes, people should not stop learning just because there are not professors. Learning gives life meaning and purpose.

To be human is to learn.

To learn is the third step to Discovering Your Human Algorithm.

----

1 Walle, E. A. (2016). Infant social development across the transition from crawling to walking. Frontiers in psychology, 7, 960.

2 Kouider, S., Stahlhut, C., Gelskov, S. V., Barbosa, L. S., Dutat, M., de Gardelle, V., ... & Dehaene-Lambertz, G. (2013). A neural marker of perceptual consciousness in infants. Science, 340(6130), 376-380.

3 Iterative = repeating; making repetition; repetitious. "Iterative" is often used in scientific circles and research and development circles to talk about how through trial and error new discoveries are made.

4 the substitution of the name of an attribute or adjunct for that of the thing meant, for example suit for business executive, or the track for horse racing.

Art

To be human is to create.

As humans, we are born to create.

With learning, new ways and forms emerge: Art.

The fourth A stands for Art and its order in the 6As is important. Though engaging in Art is sometimes dismissed as frivolous, it is Art that serves as a cornerstone to Discovering Your Human Algorithm. Art incorporates Athletics, Adventure, and Academics because each is required to engage in creative activities.

For example, filmmakers on a set of a movie have to engage in physically demanding chores for 16 hours daily for weeks on end in order to meet the demands required by producers. This grueling production schedule, even when well planned, will require that filmmakers (directors, directors of photography, gaffers, sound people, writers, actors, stunt people, caterers, wardrobe and makeup people, editors, and others) solve countless problems with sometimes no apparent reason or end in sight. Not everyone is willing to engage in this type of madness just to place images side by side on a timeline that then move from one image to the next for 120 minutes.

Beyond the physical and problem-solving demands, filmmakers have to apply intelligence, craft, and skill to each activity. The writer has to bricolage a compelling story in compelling visual form while keeping track of character arcs. The director must mix compassion for actors and crew while minding the budget of the people who pay for the movie. The director of photography needs to ensure that the lighting and shot angles are clean while managing a crew of people dedicated to the service of the technical requirements of the camera. The actors must rehearse their lines then deliver them as if they have never said them before understanding how their character serves the story. The editor must ensure that there is continuity in look and feel from one shot to the next to cobble together a story that's compelling and watchable. Filmmakers combine grueling days that require problem-solving and application of knowledge, in order to develop something new, novel, distinct, entertaining, or inspirational. It is something that we can call Art.

Art Definitions

Art is the application of human creative skill. It involves using aesthetic principles to create something more than the normal, ordinary, or usual. "Something more" includes visual arts, literature, and performing arts. In Discovering Your Human Algorithm, Art is the application of new or novel approaches to any task. This expansive definition allows people to access and experience the best of themselves. Like with the other As, the goal of engaging in Art is to derive the most from human experience at any moment.

Art in other forms

Think of a mountain climber who decides to climb his favorite trail one morning. He knows the route to get to the base of the mountain and he knows many of the techniques to help him advance as he carries a backpack of equipment. Still, his climb is Art because like a painter with an idea that hasn't yet been executed, the climber has to complete the climbs with precision and improv. The further he climbs the more refined his movements become. Eventually he arrives at his campground for the night and like a maestro who doesn't waste one single movement he has elevated his Adventure to an Artistic endeavor.

A nephrologist is a doctor who deals with complications of the kidneys, the organs tasked with removing waste and excess fluid from blood. Many nephrologists combine the skills of a data analyst with a chemist because the tools of their trade are to understand multiple thresholds of chemical counts to make decisions about patient treatment. They can talk for hours about what each blood measurement means and how each of these measures relates to kidney function and the downstream effects on the body.

But if you decide to ask a nephrologist about the latest treatment, the cutting edge of science and treatment, at some point the nephrologist may say something like "this is the state of the art we know." Scientists and doctors use this terminology — state of the art —

when what they objectively know comes into contact with the unknown. It is at this point that medicine becomes like Art, the exploration of the unknown based on principles of the known.

On an early, cool morning, a group of food bank volunteers shows up ready. They stand in line to enter the warehouse where they will be creating packages for people short on food. They shuffle in and find that coffee and donuts have been put out for them. After a few minutes someone greets them to instruct them on the 20 pieces that will go into the box and the order in which each piece needs to be placed into the box. Volunteers are assigned various stations and they begin to work. The coordination among the volunteers lifting, packing, and passing the materials takes form. With a drone's view, we would witness an unfolding of symmetrical and dynamic beauty; poetry in motion. Art manifests in life like Fibonacci sequences: 1, 1, 2, 3, 5, 8 revealing nature's underlying beauty.

Art as Adventure

Art is like Adventure. In the same time, it takes to watch a show on Netflix, you can go for a hike. Binge watching Netflix is passive. Going for a hike requires active engagement. Art similarly means that during your snooze time in the morning, you could play with positive and negative space. In vision, positive space refers to the main focus of the picture or the foreground. Negative space refers to the background. The foreground of an image is prominent while the background adds to and supports the principal focus.

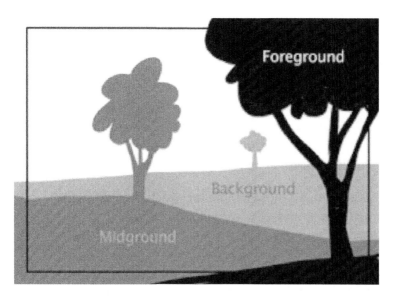

Image 5: Example of foreground, midground, and background (study.com).

The second you apply a pen stroke to a blank piece of paper you begin to play with positive and negative space. Doodling, drawing, or coloring is an easy way to interact with elements of the world for aesthetic affect.

In music, the same concepts of positive and negative space can be applied. For example, temporal silence (Jaworski, 1997) exemplifies negative space and it occurs when the musician introduces silence after a melody (positive space).

In film editing, telling a visual story requires changing from a scene that takes place at night to a scene that takes place during the day. This change from dark to light and the change from light to dark replicates what our eyes do when we blink (Murch, 1992). Discovering Your Human Algorithm requires that you engage in activities that involves playing with the elements of life.

Participating in Art is a full expression of being human. It doesn't mean you have to be good at it to reap its benefits. John loved painting. He had never studied it, but he always admired it from a distance. One day, he decided to go to the store and buy a canvas, brushes, and paint. How hard can it be? What he painted was by any measure amateurish with thick uneven lines, mismatched colors, no clear perspective, or point of view. He was not good. Sometimes in life you're just not very good at things. But it is through effort that you can appreciate the abilities of another. In John's case, he developed a deeper appreciation for painting because making paint come to life on canvas required extraordinary skill.

Art like Adventure means that you assemble the world in a different way. Think about sculptures and Art installations in your city and how they seemingly add nothing. Yet people crowd around these installations to take selfies. The next time you see a giant metallic orange slice next to a bike path think how the installation of something aesthetic changes the immediate space and how people interact with it. Art districts create economic value by moving time and space. And Art pays. According to the U.S. Bureau of Economic Analysis (BEA), Arts contributed more than 760 billion to the US economy in 2015. Art creates markets where once there were abandon warehouses.

Art as Practical Metaphor

Art serves as a practical and usable metaphor for Academic research as often times the person engaged in Academics is exploring space without a clear objective. For example, a researcher in an optics1 lab may look to have everything under control with sophisticated graphical representations of statistical models on multiple computer monitors and touchpad panels that control 3D microscopes, polygon scanners, and laser spectrometers. Underneath the mask of control, however, the researcher has spent all night calibrating one of the tools and somehow stumbled across a method without which the entire experiment could not succeed. Once this method is documented, it may look tidy and organized but much of science is Artistic exploration of time and space on task.

Art serves as a practical and usable metaphor for entrepreneurs who are trying to solve problems that are under-defined but instinctually precise. For example, an entrepreneur may be bothered by low educational standards in her school district. To address this issue, she decides to create a non-profit school raising money privately through friends and family. She has never started a school before or raised money before, but after finding success then applying for a state-grant that helps schools like hers, she is able to provide better education to kids and families most in need. At each step, the entrepreneur is like a sketch artist in front a terrifyingly blank piece of paper. At each step, she turns blank paper into papier-mâché.

Art serves as a practical and usable metaphor for athletes. Think of an ice skater who has trained relentlessly for years to perfect the axel jump that requires preparation, take-off, lift-off, rotation, and landing. Though each move is very mechanical, the ice skater herself elevates these coordinated movements into something we call Art.

Art expresses an ephemeral and practical application of the first three As – Athletics, Adventure, and Academics and engaging in Art is fundamental to Developing Your Human Algorithm.

Art Therapy

The idea that Art has applications beyond aesthetics has long been known. Art therapy combines knowledge of psychological theories and human development with creative processes such as drawing, painting, sculpting, or coloring to help people improve their well-being (Psychology Today, 2016). It is primarily a non-verbal approach to exploring oneself with the goal of examining one's emotions.

But why does Art have to be limited to therapy?

Art in your daily life

How do you create Art in your daily life? Simply picking up a pencil to draw, or downloading a music app to make sounds, using a scrap of paper to make origami, or doing a pas de bourrée (back-side-front dance movement) around the corner can count as engaging in Art. To be human is to explore symmetry and asymmetry and to fashion new combinations. After all the probability of your existence is more than 1 in quadrillion. That is 1 followed by 15 zeros. You are quite literally a piece of Art.

To be human is to create.

To create is the fourth step to Discovering Your Human Algorithm.

----

1 Optics is the branch of physics that studies light.

Advocacy

To be human is to help others.

As humans, we are born to help each other.

With life comes responsibility to yourself and others:
Advocacy.

The fifth A stands for Advocacy. Until now Athletics, Adventure, Academics, and Art

have focused on the individual. While improving oneself is always a worthy goal, one of the overall aims Discovering Your Human Algorithm involves improving life on earth in the 21st century. This starts with one plus another.

Advocacy refers to using our abilities to help others.

Hollywood and Advocacy

In Hollywood there's an expression that captures how to be successful in the movie business.

Question: How do you make a small fortune in Hollywood?

Answer: Start with a large fortune.

This pithy phrase captures the importance of prior success in current endeavors. By almost every sociological and statistical measure one's success is closely connected to the multiple support systems.

Tom Cruise is often held up as an example of how a person can arrive in Hollywood and become successful. It's a wonderful story. Unfortunately, it tends to overshadow the reality for the majority of actors who don't "make it." Like birds who follow migration patterns, Hollywood actors have long migrated to Southern California in January. They are "hot," "new," "fresh face," and "young." Many of them learn the hustle quickly by taking classes, auditioning, getting professional headshots, looking for an agent, and finding jobs where they can be "noticed" such as getting jobs as waiters in West Hollywood, Santa Monica, Beverley Hills, Studio City, Toluca Lake, or Encino.

Some of these actors will be cast in small parts in movies. During my eight years in Hollywood, I had numerous parts in small moves, 10 of which ended up on imdb.com. A few actors will land national television commercials. But the majority of these actors will never make it.

One key ingredient that's missing for these actors is that few have connections with or in or to "the business." That means few break in. Like most industries, the talent pool comes from a small subset of networks which are weirdly penetrable and often obscure. A majority of Ivy League students come from a small subset of high schools. In Hollywood, you have an advantage if you attend high school in Santa Monica, Beverley Hills, or Encino and if you are related to someone affiliated with one of the big five Studios: Walt Disney Pictures, Warner Bros., Universal Pictures, Columbia Pictures, or Paramount Pictures. You can take almost any profession and see that successful people often had the support of others.

Advocacy Definition

Why Advocacy?

For this book, I considered "Assistance" and "Aid.". Both "assistance" and "aid" also refer to the act of helping another. However, once the act is complete the word doesn't suggest further action. It names an action. It does not suggest a principle of helping someone. "Altruism," the principle and practice of helping others, comes closest to Advocacy as it embeds action and philosophy.

I chose Advocacy because it suggests a public act of support. Combining action in demonstrable way catalyzes change. But is Advocacy translatable? Translated to the five United Nations languages — Arabic, Chinese, French, Russian, and Spanish and the third most spoken language Hindi Advocacy has numerous definitions.

In Spanish, abogacía refers to the practice of being an attorney.

In Arabic, المناصرة (Al-Munasara) refers to supporting, aiding, or promoting.

In Chinese, 倡导 (Chàngdǎo) refers to the act of initiating or proposing.

In Russian, пропаганда (propaganda) refers to information or teaching.

In French, plaidoyer means to plea or to address a court of law.

In Hindi, वकालत (vakaalat) refers to the legal bar, the standard to becoming an attorney.

In each language, there is a public component for the concept of Advocacy. The public distinction is important to Discovering Your Human Algorithm because publicly supporting a position is how the world changes.

Advocacy and Change

Discovering Your Human Algorithm is a practical philosophy for living life with meaning and purpose. Underlying the daily actions incorporated in each A is change. The 21st century will see more change quicker than the already rapid 20th century. Much of this change is expected to be negative. Think about climate change, the coronavirus1, the problems caused by unequal distribution of wealth, access to health care, epidemics, and the straining and morphing of societies through the implementation and use of social media. Think

68

about how technology is revolutionizing how we live in countless ways and imagine how life will look in 2099.

Take any topic. Food. How will you eat? What will you eat? Shelter. Will we all live in tall buildings or will there be open space to enjoy? Reproduction. Will we reproduce the way we have, or will we reproduce in the lab and place restrictions on who can reproduce?

Still, conversations about change are as old as time. Likely you have come across numerous quotes on change before. I've listed a few below.

"Never doubt that a small group of thoughtful, committed, citizens can change the world. Indeed, it is the only thing that ever has."

— Margaret Mead

"The world as we have created it is a process of our thinking. It cannot be changed without changing our thinking."

— Albert Einstein

"Be the change that you wish to see in the world."

— Mahatma Gandhi

Change Requires People

While change can begin with anyone anywhere, eventually change requires a group of people. In fact, in any population 3.5% of the group can change history according to Erica Chenoweth. Working at Harvard University, Professor Chenoweth studied 323 violent and non-violent campaigns in the 20th century to determine some of the key factors for change. The result? Non-violent campaigns were twice as likely to succeed as violent campaigns.

Given these results, it suggests that change begins with you, and a small group of people around you. If you apply this idea to changing a policy in your company, an ordinance in your neighborhood, or an action your non-profit takes, then how many people does it take to make change? Let's do the math. If there are 100 people in any group, it only takes 3 or 4 of them to make a difference.

If 3.5% of the population actively participates, it ensures change. In a small city of 10,000 people, only 350 people have to be active in order to change an outcome. If we take this idea from the political sphere and apply to business, how many people did it take to help revolutionize business at Microsoft, Apple, Google, Facebook, Amazon, and other large companies?

This is not to say that change is easy. Change is hard. The powers that be always resist change because it does not benefit them … yet. Change is hard but engaging in change is powerful and positive. Social scientists have long known that those who hold positive religious and spiritual beliefs have a sunnier outlook on life (Dr. Koenig, Duke University, 2002). Literally believing in positive change is good for your health. Knowing that it takes 3.5% of the population provides empirical support that working toward positive goals can change the world. And why would we want to think otherwise? Believing in things are good provides a beneficial way to live.

Changing yourself is good. Improving the world is better. But for the work of early surgeons who risked life and reputation to perform dangerous organ transplants, but for the willingness of patients to undergo a risky operation with no guarantee of survival, but for the dedication and patience of nurses to solve countless problems with kindness, but for the daily grind of pharmaceutical professionals to experiment and create new medications, but for the hard work of hospital staff members to maintain sanitary conditions in operating rooms and recovery rooms, hundreds of thousands of people would not live to see their grandchild, travel to a new destination, launch a company, start a family, walk on the beach during sunset, or better yet, discover something new. Discovering Your Human Algorithm requires a public and community component in order to change the world. That's why Advocacy is critical to Discovering Your Human Algorithm.

Advocacy in your daily life

How do you include helping others in your daily life? Advocacy is a choice just like the other As. This can apply to a person who runs a homeless shelter, a businessperson who takes on the role of mentoring for less experienced businesspeople, or a volunteer who donates hours to helping others. The secret ingredient to Advocacy and all the other As is action. Advocacy exists as the key variable for all of lives greatest moments.

To be human is to help others.

To help others is the fifth step to Discovering Your Human Algorithm.

----

1 It's April 2020 as I write this chapter. The coronavirus dominates the news headlines.

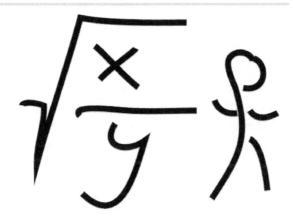

The Human Algorithm

To be human is to help improve the world.

As humans, we are born to improve life for ourselves and others.

By applying Athletics, Adventure, Academics, Art, and Advocacy we create:

The Human Algorithm.

The sixth and final A stands for The Human Algorithm. The first four As -- Athletics, Adventure, Academics, and Art -- focus on the individual. The last two As -- Advocacy and Human Algorithm – focus on the community and the greater good.

The Human Algorithm Definition

The final A of the 6As is called The Human Algorithm. I define the Human Algorithm as all the processes we conduct to learn about ourselves, master our interactions with others, and harmonize our relationship with the environment in order to live life with meaning and purpose in the 21st century.

Technology has defined our species. The invention of fire, the wheel, paper, writing, the printing press, the compass, electricity, the internal combustion engine, the telephone, vaccinations, cars, airplanes, the computer, the internet, and the use of the scientific method have propelled us along paths our ancestors may never have imagined. We swim in technology.

Yet the coronavirus has spread. Its spread has been accelerated by misinformation and poor decision making. Would more technology help slow the spread of COVID-19 and other pathogens? Yes. But what we are seeing on a world scale is that the basics of hand washing, covering our mouths, and social distancing are the greatest tools in our arsenal. They are easy and powerful to use.

However, the coronavirus has spread because of poor Human Algorithms. What do I mean by that? One of the biggest obstacles to slow the spread of the virus is how well societies adopt broad-based practices to flatten the curve. This is not rocket science. This is communication. The insurmountable problem appears to be the lack of common Human Algorithm. Group A minimizes the problems associated with the coronavirus. Group B maximizes the problems associated with the coronavirus.

Both groups operate on their assumptions no matter the facts. Both groups share their version of the facts slowing the response time which increases the speed and breadth of the coronavirus. With improved Human Algorithms, we could address the cluster of problems associated with the coronavirus more effectively.

How The Human Algorithm incorporates the other A's

The Human Algorithm encompasses all the other A's – Athletics, Adventure, Academics, Art, and Advocacy. The Human Algorithm also stands alone. It may be the most important practical philosophy to adopt for the 21st century. Before we talk about its importance, let's look at how The Human Algorithm incorporates each of the other As.

Athletics. We learned that Athletics refers to movement. As humans our primary activity first and foremost is to move. We move unconsciously. We move consciously. Our posture influences our behavior and the behavior of those around us. When we open the door for someone else who is walking in a building, we positively influence those around us. When we pick up a piece of trash and put it in a waste bin, we positively influence those around us. When we caress a loved one, we positively influence those around us. In each action, we communicate with movement and we strengthen the fabric of The Human Algorithm.

Adventure. We learned that Adventure refers to exploring new boundaries. Through movement we discover new physical places and we discover and create new neural, physical, and emotional pathways. Collectively, Adventure demonstrates to the world new possibilities. As a child, our first walk gives us a glimpse into our place and possibilities in the world. If the world is filled with countless variables, one of our tasks as humans is to begin to swim through the variables. When we apply action to a problem, we produce results. From answering our questions, we move from the known to the unknown. Each answer produces a new starting point.

It is the ever-creating starting points that allows us to participate in The Human Algorithm for ourselves and others.

Academics. We learned that Academics refers to learning new things. Reflection leads learning, and applying what we learn to new situations. After repeated Adventures, we begin to notice external and internal patterns. We notice how to categorize phenomena in similar and dissimilar stages. We can observe these phenomena and begin to draw connections and inferences between them. We can isolate and test these phenomena to produce results that give us a micro and meta sense of the world. This process teaches us, transforms us, and reveals us. This process becomes a virtuous circle of The Human Algorithm.

Art. We learned that Art refers to the playful application of things we have learned. We dance, we paint, we draw, and we build new tools. We start new projects, social ventures, and businesses. Art is sublimely and creatively assembling the unconscious and conscious things we have learned in Athletics, Adventure, and

Academics. Art takes us toward new ends that often have no clear reasons or goals. We play because we like to play. Art provides the ultimate channel to provide feedback loops to the other A's. In dance, we may stumble across a new movement and apply that to Athletics. In storytelling, we may find out that we are crazy enough to make a movie and apply that craze to Adventure. In recognizing new patterns, we may decide to try to test and isolate patterns to make new discoveries in Academics. The pursuit of Art in all its forms can be the most meaningful activity for a healthy life for ourselves and the people around us. The Human Algorithm takes full advantage of people's positive collective energies to accomplish goals to solve new problems.

Advocacy. We learned that Advocacy refers to using our abilities to help others. Advocacy builds directly from Art which borrows on the cognitive and emotional skills developed in Athletics, Adventure, and Academics. Scholars know that their work is built on the foundation of previous scholars. Sculptors push one

75

another to make ever more realistic, surrealistic, and fantastic pieces. Teammates understand that they achieve together or lose together. It is through experience in any of these and all of these that we learn to give voice to the voiceless, connection to the connectionless, power to the powerless in moments in need. We realize that we may be at the receiving end of a kind and outstretched hand who wants nothing more than to help someone else. This desire to help others is an important part of The Human Algorithm because it adds purpose, grace, and intelligence to our ability to solve problems together.

I tell my freshman psychology 101 students that some of them will see the end of the 21st century. I share this as a way for them to think about their role in the world. A few may make it. Public health trends suggest that they won't. People who are younger are dying more often from a variety of causes. Certainly, our harm of the environment is one cause. Are there more deaths younger because of our overuse of social media and our underuse of the tools that bring us joy? The Human Algorithm and our ability to serve ourselves and others is what we must effectively master quickly in order to live well together.

The Power to Change

In Discovering Your Human Algorithm, we explore how humans can re-program ourselves, how we can change behavior, and how we can change the course of history for the better.

Doubt that? Then, think about the names Jesus, Moses, Mohammed, Confucius, or Buddha and how they have changed the trajectory of human life by considering the behaviors under which people live and should live and you will appreciate the power of The Human Algorithm.

Each of these humans in history came up with a new set of practices and applied it to their time. Many of their practices became timeless because they revealed the principles that apply to the external and the internal human condition. Humans are not fundamentally different than 10,000 years ago but people at one point in time reflected on something and thought "I want the world to behave differently," "I want society to behave differently" and so they thought through a series of ideas, words, actions, and behaviors, and they changed the world fundamentally.

Think about the names Marie Curie, Susan B. Anthony, Mary Seacole, Josephine Butler and Florence Nightingaleand how they have changed the trajectory of human life by considering the behaviors under which people live and should live and you will appreciate the power of The Human Algorithm.

Still doubt that?

In the 20th century, Martin Luther King, Mahatma Gandhi, Pablo Picasso, Neil Armstrong, Muhammad Ali, Rosa Parks, Mother Teresa, Frida Kahlo, Amelia Earhart, and Billy Jean King come to mind.

In 2020, it is hard not to think of the teams of doctors, nurses, and health care professionals who work tirelessly around the world to treat people who are suffering from the coronavirus.

Who's on your list?

Human Algorithm Examples

Dr. Robert W. Fuller has had numerous lives as a physicist, academic reformer, college president, citizen diplomat, board chair, advisor to presidents and prime ministers, futurist, and prolific author.

But his work in "rankism" stands out as an exemplar of The Human Algorithm. Dr. Fuller identifies abuses of power and calls them "rankism." Another way to think about "rankism" is the assertion of authority. Usually these abuses take the names "bullying," "racism," "hazing," "ageism," "sexism," "ableism," "mentalism," "homophobia", and "transphobia."

In each case, the person who is in the more powerful position can use one of these "isms" to gain an advantage. Dr. Fuller calls these phenomena examples of "rankism." In each situation, the person asserts authority over another simply because he or she is able to in a particular circumstance.

Rankism is also multidirectional. A person who is discriminated against at work can go home at night and exhibit bullying behavior against a child. That is everyone can be bullies and victims.

I list "rankism" as an example of The Human Algorithm because it operates like a social technology. Identifying behaviors then developing new terms for them is the first step to mitigating and changing behavior. "Phubbing" identifies the rude behavior we exhibit toward one another by using our phones or electronic devices in the presence of others. We "snub" them with our phones, hence "phone + snub" equals snubbing.

This word helps identify counterproductive behavior. Naming things with the goal of improving things demonstrates an example of The Human Algorithm.

Syd Mead is a visual futurist who has helped design the visual landscapes for science fiction films such as Blade Runner, Aliens and Tron. As an industrial designer since the 1950s, he has seen massive changes in car, hotel, and movie design. Yet, one of his common refrains is that the human animal doesn't change.

Instead the human animal only switches out one satisfaction device for another. Where once there was a towel and water, now there is toothbrush and toothpaste. Where once there was once a horse-and-carriage conveyance, now there is a car. Where once there was a stage, now there is a cinema. The point that Syd Mead makes in his work that humans change little, simply the devices they use.

If each successive generation simply switches various products to define their era without improving underlying conditions, then what does it say about us? Are humans destined to repeat the same cycles of design, destruction, and recreation? Many computer programs feel like this. Auto-correct demands our attention in the most mundane texts. And we can't seem to un-auto-correct. But we march forward working with restrictions that bind us, silently complaining. Do we always ignore the annoyance of auto-correct? Is the human condition similar?

The Human Algorithm in your daily life

It is through practice of Athletics, Adventure, Academics, Art, and Advocacy that one can elevate to mastery, then apply the mastery of multiple intelligences to one's own Human Algorithm.

For example, dedicated students move along the path from skill development to application of those skills. Take a freshman student in a writing class. The first year he may struggle with grammar and sentence structure. Once he masters the fundamentals, he can begin to think about hooks, thesis statements, and topic sentences. Later he will begin to assess the audience. With all of these skills mastered through repeated practice, the student starts to become the teacher who can share the process of learning with others. If this student deftly communicates his best practices with others, then he begins to fashion a Human Algorithm that can change the life of one other person. With repeated practice, the student recognizes new patterns in writing. The student stitches together pattern recognition and builds heuristics for each pattern.

Seeing one data point, then two data points, then three leads to accurate predictions of what comes next and an uncanny ability to improv with unexpected events. This mastery is called The Human Algorithm and it comes with dedicated practice and reflection and a willingness to risk everything to do the scariest thing in life: change.

But change is the most fundamental of all principles. Whether the student who has become the master accepts it or not, she must contend with change. The evolutionary biologist knows that adaption requires that one preserves, discards, and creates. The butterfly has to start sometime. You are the butterfly. It is your Human Algorithm.

To be human is to improve.

To improve life on earth for yourself and others in the 21st century is the sixth step to Discovering Your Human Algorithm.

The Ultimate A's

To be human is to finish.

The Ultimate A is Action. Any action takes us somewhere and teaches us.

I have written Discovering Your Human Algorithm to remind you what you intuitively know. To be human is to move and discover and learn and create and help others and improve life on earth. Engaging in one or all of the 6A actions daily will focus your attention on the moment. It is the space over which you have control and it is the space from which you can develop tremendous satisfaction. Engaging in the 6As prompts learning, re-learning, and un-learning. The 6As derive from the activities I have always been drawn toward and I feel are the most important for humans to have a fulfilling life. Below I share some personal examples.

Athletics. Growing up I always played sports. I played volleyball, basketball, baseball, soccer, and I competed in bike races. My best sport was soccer which took me to Europe and eventually led to a college soccer scholarship. As an adult, I regularly compete in triathlons and international competitions. It is through Athletics that I have learned resiliency through failure. The best athletes have failed more than they have succeeded. It is through Athletics I have learned teamwork. Everyone on a team has something to contribute. Always. Learning this lesson never gets old because each configuration of humans and each situation provide new challenges.

Adventure. Adventure came naturally at an early age as we moved frequently. I attended four elementary schools, one middle school, and two high schools during my primary and secondary school years, then later I attended three colleges. When we weren't moving, we were traveling. My parents both rode motorcycles. My younger brother rode with my Dad on his 1,000 CC BMW. I rode with my Mom on her 900 CC BMW. We traveled through the western United States, an area full of large skies, wondrous landscapes, wind, and heat. We often camped out on large mountain tops and one time we even "camped out" in a hotel in Leadville, Colorado where it was so cold during September that we slept in our sleeping bags under the covers.

Another Adventure took me to Europe. At one point, I nearly got stuck in the Moscow International Airport when a Soviet guard forgot to stamp my passport. The moving and traveling that was inculcated early has become a life of Adventure.

I have had numerous "lives" (maybe not careers) as varied as working at Silicon Valley startups, pursuing acting in Hollywood, completing a PhD, working for a biotech company, and now writing a book.

Academics. I completed formal academic training, earning a PhD at a time when many people have hit their career-stride and it took me awhile with numerous failed education attempts. Here are a few. During my first semester of college at Metropolitan State College in Denver, Colorado, I failed my courses in reading and writing. Luckily, I did so poorly that none of my courses transferred to the next semester to Arapahoe Community College in Littleton, Colorado. At the Freie Universität in Berlin, Germany, I completed master's courses in political science and international law, but didn't finish. At Denver University in Denver, Colorado, I started then dropped out of a master's degree in telecommunications. At Santa Clara University in Santa Clara, California, I started then dropped out of law school where I planned to specialize in patents.

I often share my stories of failure with my students as a way to connect to them who have goals but have to overcome other hurdles first. The point of the 6As is take action. In the movie "Yes Man," a divorced man who says 'no' to every opportunity, suddenly commits to saying 'yes' to every opportunity after attending a self-help talk. Every opportunity he accepted didn't lead to immediate success but every opportunity he accepted led to ultimate satisfaction. Focusing on one or all of the 6As is a way to focus on the higher side of you.

Art. While working 14-hour days at a Silicon Valley company, I needed to find a release. Sure, my friends and I went to "The City" every weekend to dance at clubs and I thought I was one of the best, but I felt that I needed to test myself under "real" conditions. So, I signed up for a dance class. Ouch. I should list dance under Athletics because it is one of the most grueling physical activities I have ever done. I list it under Art because dance is known as a temporal art which exists only in the moment like an ice sculpture. It exists then it melts away. Its existence fades unlike a painting, a photograph, or a film that can last forever.

This foray into dance for two years led to acting. When I showed up at auditions for leading man roles, the director would usually say, "Yeah, you know, that was good, but we really like you for this other part. The character we think you can do is a little off. You're edgy." I went on to earn 10 imdb.com credits working in 38 film projects being edgy.

Advocacy. I have always had a sense of justice. For me, it's like a weathervane which is a metal object that sits on top of a building to show which way the wind is blowing. Often, I feel a wind when there is merely a breeze. While I was completing my undergraduate degree, I started the campus recycling program because I felt it was important to use our resources to their maximum potential. During the same time, I launched a youth exchange program between the United States and Germany because I wanted to contribute to peace. During my PhD studies, I served as the Graduate Student Body President for four terms because it was clear that 9,000 students could use a voice. As an organ-transplant recipient, I have lobbied Congress directly on behalf of policies that reduce waiting list times and I currently serve as a Trustee for the World Transplant Games Federation.

The Human Algorithm. Maybe it is because I have learned four languages and multiple accents that I am tuned into the various ways that humans act toward one another. Our choices can create dramatically varied outcomes both positive and negative. With all of our technology, it seems clear to me that the great technology of the 21st century will be how to manage ourselves as we interact with technology to solve problems.

As I write, most of the world has self-imposed quarantines to slow the spread of the coronavirus (COVID-19). Slowing down infection rates can flatten the curve in order to give health care systems time to deal with patients. Developing vaccines and screening tools are extremely important but just as important are the behavioral choices individuals and societies make to reduce sickness and death. Choosing wisely and informing ourselves with accurate information is an example of The Human Algorithm in the 21st century.

Putting Your Human Algorithm into Action

The 6As can be practiced daily in less than an hour. The combination of activities will help you discover Your Human Algorithm to live with meaning and purpose. To start, let's plan an hour. You will need a small backpack and some water. Each activity takes 10 minutes. First, prepare your exercise clothes and mentally locate where you can do 10 minutes of physical exercise. This can be 10 minutes of yoga, running in place for 10 minutes, lifting weights, or doing a series of core exercise. Next, mentally find a park that is near where you will compete your exercise. The park or outdoor area will be where you will complete the additional As so choose a place with Academics, Art, and Advocacy in mind. For Academics, pack a book, a notepad and a pen or pencil. For Art, make sure to have your favorite dance music or use the same notepad. Finally, bring something to pick up trash. Cleaning up around you isn't the only way to do Advocacy but it works for this example. When you're ready, begin.

Not taking breaks between exercise, adventure, learning, art, advocacy or improving yourself is critical because the easiest way to stall progress on learning is take too much time off between learning sessions. Ideally you should practice for six consecutive days. Some A's are easier to do daily than others, but it is our intention and in the consistency in the actions that makes discovering our Human Algorithm possible. Here are a few examples.

Athletics. Whether you do aerobic exercise (e.g. running) or anaerobic exercise (e.g. lifting weights), your intention and consistency are key. John has been hospitalized a few times. It always frustrates him because his workouts are interrupted. His response? He counts. He counts the tiles on floor while walking around the hospital. He sets a goal of walking 100 steps. He counts laps around a ward. Later when he has been discharged from the hospital, he often looks back on these workouts. Any workout outside of the hospital is harder, but few are as important as his hospital walks.

Each Athletic activity gives us an opportunity for the three types of learning. The hospital walks can help you learn how to refine your walk or walking stride for maximum efficiency when feeling pain. The hospital walks can help you re-learn to walk, as your mind teaches your body to move again or move more efficiently. The hospital walks can help you un-learn some bad habits that you may have acquired or developed in your gait.

Adventure. Attitude determines adventure just as much as action does. We often have a sense of admiration and envy for people who travel to the wilderness for a "backpacking Adventure" or people who travel frequently because their actions provide a clear visual of Adventure. But Adventure is the desire to see the world in a new way so that intention + action can mean Adventure. For example, a person who is diagnosed with cancer faces difficult choices and has to deal with real life-and-death decisions along with the emotional and social impact of the diagnosis. However, many people find a sense of Adventure in the process of treatment.

Of course, we don't wish poor health for one other, but during treatment and while climbing mountains we are given the opportunity to learn, re-learn, and un-learn on a daily basis. We can learn about how well we deal with crisis despite of and then because of our moments of difficulty. We can re-learn how to find a little extra strength to push ourselves farther when we thought we had nothing left. We can also un-learn behaviors that don't help ourselves or others.

Academics. Some of the best learners have incomplete or no degrees. A film editor in Los Angeles spends her free time reading books to prepare for her next documentary and she enrolls in online courses monthly in subjects ranging from web design to chemistry. Academics can be the formal study of a subject. But Academics can be defined as curiosity combined with action. We can learn anything, anywhere, anytime online. We can learn anything, anywhere, anytime with technologies as basic as a paper and pen.

The three ways of learning are obvious in Academics. We learn new things. We re-learn concepts that we may have forgotten. We can un-learn ways of thinking that no longer serve us.

For example, for people who study decision making much of their studies involve studying mistakes and poor choices. Studying bad decisions gives us ample opportunities to un-learn behaviors that while are easy to acquire may ultimately not serve our best interests.

Art. People who study culture talk about the difference between Big C and little c. Big C is considered "formal culture" that includes the study of institutions, historical figures, literature, fine arts, and science. Little c is associated with perspectives. It is also associated with daily living which includes our housing, clothing, food, tools, transportation, and patterns of behavior.6 With that distinction in mind, it is much easier to practice Art daily. Doing any type of Art is the chance to attach spirit to action. Creating makes the human animal unique.

Doing Art gives people the chance to learn something new, often about themselves and their own ability to create something without judgment. Often through participating in Art we have the chance to re-learn something about who and how we are. And through Art we have the chance to un-learn bad habits we may have acquired elsewhere.

Advocacy. Of all of the As, Advocacy may seem like the hardest to practice because it requires at least one other human. Does Advocacy mean volunteering in some way? It can mean volunteering for charity, signing a petition, or attending an event for a cause you believe in. But it may also be as simple as speaking up for your child's well-being during a doctor's appointment or speaking up for a co-worker during a meeting. Whatever the action, Advocacy is the human spirt saying We can do something better.

Advocacy often prompts the strongest reactions which makes learning more dynamic. Most people have been in a situation in which they advocated for something and watched the reaction of others. Often times the reaction isn't positive which is why many people choose comfort over confrontation. That is understandable but most major human advances are because someone advocated for a cause or a group of people.

Advocacy acts as a challenge to the status quo which provides the opportunity to a) learn how people react, b) re-learn or at least re-consider your principles when faced with a challenge, and c) un-learn how to react when faced with a challenge. That is, if you are normally non-confrontational, maybe you un-learn to avoid confrontation to speak up for yourself in the face of a challenge. If you are normally confrontational, maybe you learn how to take deep breaths and smile when faced with a confrontation.

The Human Algorithm. The Human Algorithm refers to decisions and behaviors we make as individuals and that affect us and others. The way we treat each other has radically changed our human history for the worse and for the better. The Magna Carta signed in 1215 by King John of England gave rebellious barons a voice and it was one of the early milestones of agreed-upon behavior that lead to better treatment between those with more power and those with less power. It has launched thousands similar agreements for 800 years.

The Declaration of Human Rights in 1948 marked another milestone of a decision and dedication to recognize rights of humans everywhere. It is these Human Algorithms that can change the world. In fact, they have. If you wonder if this is true, think about how Siddhartha Gautama (Buddhism), Jesus Christ (Christianity), Muhammad (Islam), Moses known in Hebrew Moshe Rabbenu (Judaism), Confucius from the Chinese Kǒng Zi (Confucianism) changed the trajectory of human life by considering the behaviors under which people live and should live and you will appreciate the power of The Human Algorithm.

Marie Curie, Susan B. Anthony, Mary Seacole, Josephine Butler and Florence Nightingale have changed the trajectory of human life by considering the behaviors under which people live and should live and you will appreciate the power of The Human Algorithm.

Discovering Your Human Algorithm in under 60 minutes daily

1.   Complete 10-minutes of exercise. Athletics

2.   Walk in a new location or take new route 10 minutes. Adventure

3.   Read a book or write in a journal for 10 minutes. Academics

4.   Draw, doodle, color or dance for 10 minutes. Art

5.   Pick up errant items and put it in the nearest receptacle. Advocacy

6.   Take 10 minutes to reflect, then make 1 decision on how to improve life for yourself and others today. The Human Algorithm

Being positive is the only practical way to live

Discovering Your Human Algorithm means that you recognize the mini miracles of life. Discovering Your Human Algorithm means that you recognize that change comes from action.

The easiest choice to make is the negative one which is good only when identifying problems. The harder choice, but the choice that exemplifies our Human Algorithm, is the choice to incorporate the 6As into our life on a daily basis.

One of the themes of the book is about choosing positive, thoughtful actions in the face of negativity. The theme embeds the idea that we can choose to see the best in each other despite "evidence." I'm not pollyannaish. "Losses loom larger than gains"1 but our ability to see the light in the dark is our greatest repeatable traits. During our shared coronavirus experience, we see daily examples of people rising to the occasion and creating better Human Algorithms.

Discovering Your Human Algorithm. How to Live with Meaning and Purpose is a practical philosophy designed to help us improve life on earth in the 21st century.

As my Dad once said, "being positive is the only practical way to live."

----

1 Kahneman & Tversky, 1979

Additional Thanks

randomized order

Ultimate A: About the Author

In his first book, Discovering Your Human Algorithm -- How to Live with Meaning and Purpose, Dr. Zachary S. Brooks draws upon his experiences as college and international athlete (played soccer in Europe) traveler (visited 25 countries and speaks 4 languages), academic (hooded in the College of Science and Humanities), Hollywood Actor (10 credits on imdb.com), organ donation advocate (Trustee for World Transplant Games Federation) to share tips on living life with meaning and purpose in 18-minute segments daily.

Additional Materials

Post a Review
As a self-help author, your reviews are not only welcomed, they are important for Amazon's eBook rankings. Please take 3-5 minutes to leave a review.

Feedback & Contact
Have feedback or want to contact me? Email me at zach@discoveringyourhumanalgorithm.com.

Follow Me
Website: DiscoveringYourHumanAlgorithm.com
Facebook: Facebook.com/DiscoveringYourHumanAlgorithm
Instagram: Instagram.com/DiscoveringYourHumanAlgorithm

Newsletter Signup
http://eepurl.com/gkUTXr

Your Daily A! Your practical guide for living with meaning and purpose!
https://zachary-s-brooks.thinkific.com/

Audio Book available! Check Amazon.

Printed in Great Britain
by Amazon